BUDDY
Comes to Breakfast

Written and Illustrated by

Dee Marvin Emeigh

Sometimes friends live far away —

It was my first trip to Nevada to visit my friend, who had moved there from the east coast. The desert exhaled heat as we made our way to the car in the airport parking garage.

On our way to her house, we passed through a heavy thunder shower that quickly puddled the roadways and slowed the traffic.

"I can't remember the last time it rained," Amelie said. "Especially this time of year."

By the time we arrived at her villa, the rain had stopped and the moon was rising. She showed me to the guest room and we talked a little while before saying, "Good night."

But friends are friends,
both night and day.

Friends can live in places high.

Friends can live in places dry.

In the morning, still tired from traveling, I was eager for a cup of coffee, and to talk about the day's plans.

"Are you ready to meet Buddy?" Amelie inquired.

"I'm still in my pajamas," I laughed. I had no idea who Buddy was, but I wasn't sure I wanted to meet him in my pajamas.

"It's alright. He won't mind," she replied, looking anxiously at the clock. "I'm surprised he's not here yet." She started to cut some raw broccoli and mixed some green, mushy stuff. She placed it on a ceramic dish, opened the patio door, and brought it out to the patio table.

I watched her curiously, as she walked to the back of the courtyard where a fountain splashed water into a small pool. Then, she crouched down to look behind a rock.

"I'm a little worried," she confessed. "He doesn't like the habitat I had built for him, so he digs his own little burrow, but it's not as safe, and with the rain we had yesterday, I just hope it didn't fill up with water." She scooped away wet, sandy soil to make sure there was a clear opening.

Here in the Mojave Desert the rain was very much needed, but it was obvious that Amelie was concerned. When the rain mixed with the sandy soil, she told me, it created a cement-like mixture.

Sometimes friends live in outdoor spaces.

"Buddy, are you in there?" Amelie called.

"Yep. He's in there," she assured me.

"Let's go sit at the table and see if he'll come." A few minutes later, she turned her head and nodded toward the stone pathway beyond the fountain.

"Here he comes!"

I watched in wonder as a small, brown tortoise came creeping steadily toward us, holding my breath as he teetered over the garden hose on the way.

"You're covered with mud!" Amelie exclaimed.

"I hope he doesn't get sick," she fretted.

"You're not blowing bubbles, are you?" she asked him.

I soon learned that if Buddy had been blowing bubbles from his nose or mouth, it would mean he'd caught a cold. Thankfully, he seemed fine.

Amelie placed the dish of broccoli florets and mush on the patio floor, and Buddy moved quickly toward his food, and just as quickly into my heart.

There was so much more I wanted to learn about him.

Sometimes friends have muddy faces.

The habitat Amelie had built for Buddy in her back yard was quite safe, but Buddy didn't seem to agree. He felt safer in a smaller space that he could snuggle into; one just big enough for his shell, so he had decided to make his own burrow. He was very good at digging with his sharp claws.

When the heavy rain came, his burrow walls had begun to crumble around him and his shell, neck, and feet were now caked with caliche mud. As this clay-like soil dries, it becomes stiff and hard like rock.

In the wild, this could have been a problem, but not for Buddy. Amelie watched over her little hatchling very carefully. So, when Buddy came to breakfast at precisely 7:30 the next morning, she decided it was time to give Buddy a bath...

I watched as she filled the bird bath in her yard with water from the hose, making sure it wasn't too warm. Then she picked Buddy up by the edges of his shell and held him along the surface of the water scooping water over his back. He didn't seem to mind.

Amelie soaked the caliche-crusted areas and rubbed them gently. Then, she submerged Buddy for a few seconds and he pulled his head into his shell, because he was surprised.

Finally, when he was all clean, she carefully placed him back on the ground to let him eat his breakfast.

His shell was beautiful!

HOLLYHOCK 15¢
ANNUAL INDIAN SPRING
F. LAGOMARSINO & SONS
SACRAMENTO, CALIFORNIA
Lago CALIFORNIA Seeds

Friends can grow like pretty flowers.

Things Buddy Likes to Eat

One thing Buddy really likes to eat is Aloe. The Aloe plant in this sketch was rooted from one that Amelie's aunt gave her more than 40 years ago. Buddy could live much longer than that! Some Desert Tortoises live more than 80 years!

All the plants in this sketch are succulents. They contain water, a necessity for the desert animals. The sketch also shows Haworthia, Globe Mallow, and my personal favorite: Mexican Evening Primrose.

Friends can make us smile for hours.

Buddy's shell is designed with yellow-orange hexagonal shapes outlined by rings that tell a story about his age and health. His skin, which he allows his friends to touch without pulling back, is leathery. He has a very good sense of smell and his pretty pink tongue helps him decide if he likes the taste of things. The succulents and flowers he eats hydrate him, but he also drinks water.

His ears are covered with skin flaps, but Buddy can still hear very well. He could hear when Amelie called. He also sees quite well and is attracted to brightly colored objects, like painted toenails! If Buddy turns out to be a girl, her own back toenails will be longer, but it will take almost five years to determine whether Buddy is male or female.

Among other distinctions between the sexes, males have longer tails, and a larger gular horn under their chins. Whatever the sex, researchers now think that it is determined by the temperature at which the eggs were incubated.

Friends may come for a bite to eat.

When I went back to visit Buddy the following summer, he walked right up to the camera to say hello. The next day he came toward me again and continued following me around the patio for a while. Buddy spent over an hour wandering around after he ate an aloe leaf. I think he liked having me there! He enjoyed exploring my camera, and he especially liked my sandals.

As the sun began to rise, along with the temperature, reaching 85° F by 10:00 am, Buddy began to stay in the shade. At one point, he and Lila the cat were both under the barbecue grill, but when Lila saw that I'd discovered her, she moved to a new location and Buddy followed.

He can move pretty quickly when he wants to!

Buddy circled around the patio, across an area of stone and back to the shadow of the house, trying to get to his favorite spot behind the storage chest from the opposite side. When he discovered that his shell was too wide for the opening, he backed up and turned around, pausing with his head under the rim of a planter long enough for me to get a quick sketch of him. We were both hot and I figured if I didn't distract him any longer, he would find his way back to his corner behind the chest to stay cool and sheltered until later in the day.

Desert Tortoises, I learned, like all other tortoises and turtles, are ectothermic. They depend on their environment to regulate their body temperature.

Friends may even tickle our feet!

Things I learned about Buddy from watching him:

- He eats the weeds, but doesn't seem to like them much
- He loves the juicy aloe
- He uses his feet and claws to hold stems and leaves so he can rip away the tender bites he wants.
- He tries to taste everything, including toes and little stones between the pavers.

Because Buddy didn't like his man-made habitat, when it was very hot out, Amelie brought him inside the house and put him in a large tray with an upside down box for him to crawl into, so he was safe and secure. In the winter, keeping him safe meant bringing him in to a safe, dark, quiet spot where it was cool.

In fact, Buddy spent the winter months in Amelie's garage in a banker's box with a few inches of caliche soil covering the bottom. A burrow under the ground will usually stay around 55° F, so Amelie also placed a thermometer in the box to make sure it wasn't too cold.

When Buddy tried to taste my foot, I discovered his mouth was sharp and hard like a bird's beak. It pinched! I guess when he gets bigger, that could be a problem, so I won't let him do that again.

Friends can come in many sizes.

Like every young creature, Buddy will be growing, and how much or how little he grows is an indication of how healthy he is. So, Amelie keeps a record of his weight.

When he woke up from brumation, he weighed less than when he went to sleep. This is because he did not eat or drink anything during that time, which can be as long as four months. Over the next four months, however, Buddy had a very good appetite! From March to July, he almost doubled his weight. He ate his tortoise-diet food mix a few times each week as well as some occasional broccoli florets and aloe.

Some days, Amelie let Buddy find his own food around the courtyard. She has planted her yard with things Buddy likes, so he can find them on his own. This is important, because Buddy should be able to forage independently in case he has to be on his own for a few days.

When Amelie weighed Buddy this year, he was too heavy for the food scale, so she had to do some math. She weighed herself and then held Buddy and weighed herself again. The added weight was Buddy's. He weighed one pound!

As Buddy grows, his shell grows with him. The spaces between his beautiful gold hexagons fill in.

Friends can be full of surprises!

October 2013

Amelie tells me that as the days get shorter, Buddy comes to breakfast later and later.

August 2014

Amelie says she looked all over the yard and could not find Buddy, so she got a flashlight and checked inside the habitat... After almost two years, Buddy finally went in all by himself. She's hoping he will spend the winter in there, instead of in the garage!

Friends are always glad we're there.

Friends show friends they really care.

In the summer of 2015, I went to see Buddy for the last time. Amelie was planning to move back east, but Buddy needed to stay in Nevada to survive. Although she was sad to have to leave Buddy behind, Amelie knew that was what was best for her friend. He is a very friendly little tortoise with a distinctive personality, and he will be adopted again.

He noticed me right away at the window, so I went out and took pictures of him eating his breakfast. Then, he investigated my sandals again. The following morning, he showed me how he was now living in his habitat. He came out and stopped by the opening for a minute, looking up at the statue of the large tortoise carrying the small one.

"That's what friends do," he seemed to say. "They help each other and do what's best for each other."

Friends will do for friends what's best.

Buddy's backyard paradise has
Grapevines, Hollyhocks, Mexican
Evening Primrose, Globe Mallow,
Silver Falls Dichondra, a shallow
waterfall, and plenty of room for
him to grow.

To have a friend is to be blessed!

28

home
7-14-14

TAD - Buddy has a cousin named Tad who is 30 years old! He lives on the other side of town and has his own habitat and yard.

Tad comes out of his habitat when his caretaker calls him.

He is quite a bit bigger than Buddy.

Tad likes to eat

- yellow earth roses
- hibiscus flowers
- grape leaves

and of course, his special diet mix.

MORE INFORMATION ON THE DESERT TORTOISE

The following websites and organizations have lots more information on the Desert Tortoise, adoption, and growing foraging food:

Adopting -
http://www.ndow.org/Desert-Tortoise-Adoption-Available-Throughout-Nevada/

Answering Questions about Desert Tortoises A Guide for People Who Work with the Public - K. H. Berry & T. Duck - http://www.deserttortoise.org/answeringquestions/chapter1.html

Facts and a booklet of Frequently Asked Questions (pdf) - http://www.fws.gov/nevada/desert_tortoise/dt/dt_pet.html

National Park Service information webpage about the Desert Tortoise and its plight -
http://www.nps.gov/jotr/learn/nature/tortoise.htm

Seeds to plant for Desert Tortoise foraging -
http://www.desertseedstore.com/category/Tortoise-Forage-Seed-Mixes-Edibles-76

Tortoise Group, a non-profit educational and advocacy group for the protection and well-being of the Desert Tortoise -
https://www.tortoisegroup.org/

WORDS TO KNOW ABOUT BUDDY AND HIS COUSINS

Brumate - The prolonged sluggish inactivity of reptiles during extended periods of cool weather; like hibernation in warm-blooded animals.

Caliche soil - Sand or clay soil with high content of crystalline salts such as sodium nitrate or sodium chloride.

Carapace - The shell covering the back or dorsal side of tortoises.

Chelonian - A turtle or being turtle like.

Ectothermic - Describing an animal that regulates its body temperature mostly by exchanging heat with its surrounding environment.

Gopherus Agassizii - The scientific name for the Desert Tortoise, named after scientist Louis Agassiz.

Gular horn - The part of the shell that extends out from under the tortoise's head. Larger in males.

Herpetology - The branch of zoology dealing with reptiles and amphibians.

Plastron - The under, or belly side of the shell.

Predators of young Desert Tortoises include Ravens and Roadrunners, Foxes, Snakes, Bobcats, Badgers, and Coyotes. These stones in Amelie's yard are a good camoflage for Buddy. He's hidden in plain sight!

"Everyone Needs a Hand"

If you enjoyed Buddy Comes to Breakfast, you may also like to have a copy of this fine art photographic print of Buddy, available in various formats and sizes from:
http://bit.ly/BuddysBath